Charlie Brown's 'Cyclopedia
has been produced
by Mega-Books of New York,
Inc. in conjunction
with the editorial, design,
and marketing staff of
Field Publications.

**STAFF FOR
MEGA-BOOKS**

Pat Fortunato
Editorial Director

Diana Papasergiou
Production Director

Susan Lurie
Executive Editor

Rosalind Noonan
Senior Editor

Adam Schmetterer
Research Director

**Michaelis/Carpelis
Design Assoc., Inc.**
Art Direction and Design

**STAFF FOR
FIELD PUBLICATIONS**

Cathryn Clark Girard
Assistant Vice President,
Juvenile Publishing

Elizabeth Isele
Executive Editor

Kristina Jones
Executive Art Director

Leslie Erskine
Marketing Manager

Elizabeth Zuraw
Senior Editor

Michele Italiano-Perla
Group Art Director

Kathleen Hughes
Senior Art Director

Photograph and Illustration Credits:
American Museum of Natural History, 16, 17, 38; Animals Animals/Hans and Judy Beste, 49; Animals Animals/W. Gregory Brown, 26; Animals Animals/M.A. Chappell, 33; Animals Animals/Bruce Davidson, 28; Animals Animals/Michael Fogden, 37; Animals Animals/Zig Leszczynski, 21, 25, 26, 27; Animals Animals/Terry Murphy, 45; Animals Animals/Robert Pearcy, 45; Animals Animals/Maresa Pryor, 9, 19; Animals Animals/Leonard Lee Rue III, 22, 31; Animals Animals/Len Rue Jr., 48; "THE BOOK OF THE DEAD", Copyright © 1960 by University Books, Inc. Published by arrangement with Carol Publishing Group, 53; Jim Brandenburg/West Light, 30; David Celsi, 13, 15, 18, 22, 24, 54, 55; Diagram Visual Information Ltd., 11; Earth Scenes/Breck P. Kent, 15; Charles R. Knight/American Museum of Natural History, 12, 37, 39; Chuck O'Rear/West Light, 28; Brian Vikander/West Light, 42, 47; William J. Warren/West Light, 18.

ISBN: 0-8374-0047-3

Part of the material in this volume was previously published in *Charlie Brown's Second Super Book of Questions and Answers*.

Funk & Wagnalls, founded in 1876, is the publisher of *Funk & Wagnalls New Encyclopedia,* one of the most widely owned home and school reference sets, and many other adult and juvenile educational publications.

INTRODUCTION

Welcome to volume 2 of *Charlie Brown's 'Cyclopedia!* Have you ever wondered why the dinosaurs disappeared, why birds sing, or what "playing possum" means? Charlie Brown and the rest of the *Peanuts* gang are here to help you find the answers to these questions and many more about some of the most fascinating animals on Earth. Have fun!

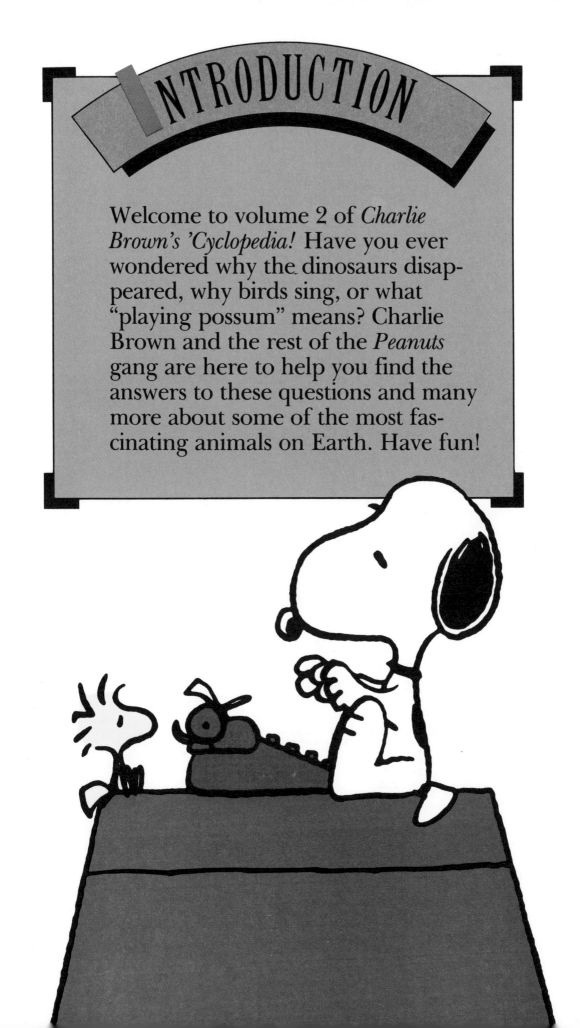

CONTENTS

The ground trembled under their heavy footsteps. Huge and mighty, they roamed the Earth—maybe even in your neighborhood. That was about 200 million to 60 million years ago. Who were these giant creatures? They were reptiles that we have named dinosaurs!

WHEN DINOSAURS WALKED THE EARTH

THE EARLIEST REPTILES

What is a reptile?

The word *reptile* means that which crawls. A reptile is an animal that crawls, though some prefer to swim. Reptiles usually have scales on their bodies, like fish, but they breathe through lungs, as people do. Reptiles are cold-blooded. This means that the temperature of their blood changes when the air temperature changes. Snakes, turtles, and lizards are all reptiles. So were the ancient dinosaurs.

The smallest dinosaurs were about the size of chickens. The biggest, nose to tail, were as long as a ten-story building is high!

What were dinosaurs like?

When dinosaurs first appeared, there were not yet any birds or furry animals on Earth. But there were many kinds of dinosaurs in all sorts of shapes and sizes. Some lived on land, and others mostly stayed in the water. Some dinosaurs walked on two legs, and others walked on all four of their legs. There were dinosaurs that ate meat and dinosaurs that ate only plants. Many dinosaurs had a tough plate of armor covering their bodies. This armor helped protect the dinosaurs from enemies.

What does *dinosaur* mean?

The word *dinosaur* means terrible lizard. However, scientists have learned that some dinosaurs looked more like birds than lizards. We think that some of the dinosaurs *were* terrible and fierce. Others were quieter and more peaceful creatures.

Were there people living at the same time as dinosaurs?

No. Dinosaurs died out millions of years before the first humans appeared on Earth. No person has ever seen a living dinosaur. We know how they looked from their bones and from imprints they left in rock.

WHY THE DINOSAURS DISAPPEARED

Why did dinosaurs die out?

No one is sure why dinosaurs died out—became "extinct"—but there are a few possible reasons. One is that the climate of the world changed. The warm, wet places where the dinosaurs lived became drier and cooler. This colder weather killed the plants that some of the dinosaurs ate. When the plants died, the plant-eaters starved. When the plant-eating dinosaurs died, so did the meat-eating dinosaurs—since they ate the plant-eaters.

We know that other kinds of animals appeared on Earth before dinosaurs became extinct. These new animals may have caused the dinosaurs to die out. The animals may have eaten dinosaur eggs. If the eggs were all eaten, there would be no new dinosaurs. Or perhaps the new animals ate the same food as the dinosaurs, and the dinosaurs could no longer find enough to eat.

Another possible reason for the death of the dinosaurs is that they could have been struck down by a deadly, world-wide disease.

COLLECTING DINOSAUR FACTS

How do we collect facts about dinosaurs?

We know how dinosaurs looked, what they ate, how they walked, and many other things—all because we have found their bones and other remains of their bodies. These remains lay buried in the Earth for millions of years and slowly turned to stone. They are called fossils. The word *fossil* means dug up.

Here's a fossil of a dinosaur found in Germany.

The largest number of dinosaur remains in North America have been found in Colorado!

When were the first dinosaur fossils found?

The first dinosaur fossils were found about 175 years ago in Connecticut. Since then, a great many others have been found in other parts of the world. These fossils are mainly dinosaur bones, teeth, and eggs. Scientists can put the bones together into whole skeletons, and from the skeletons they can tell what dinosaurs actually looked like. By studying fossil teeth, scientists can tell whether a dinosaur ate plants or meat. Meat-eaters had pointed, sharp teeth for tearing meat. Dinosaurs that ate plants had flat, blunt teeth, designed for chewing.

Other dinosaur fossils are footprints in the earth that have turned to stone. From these, scientists can tell how a dinosaur walked and how heavy it was.

What colors were dinosaurs?

One thing no one knows about dinosaurs is what color they were. Scientists have found prints of dinosaur skin in stone, but the prints are the color of the fossil stone—not of the dinosaur.

15

DIFFERENT TYPES OF DINOSAURS

If you lived around 200 million years ago, you might have seen these dinosaurs.

ALLOSAUR

Which were the largest dinosaurs?

When seismosaurus (sighs-mo-SORE-us) was discovered in 1986, some scientists thought that this was the largest dinosaur. It grew to be nearly 150 feet long. More recently, a scientist studying fossil bones of different large dinosaurs discovered another dinosaur, a supersaurus (super-SORE-us). Although it was not as long as seismosaurus, supersaurus probably weighed about 67 tons. Compare that to an elephant, which weighs about 7½ tons, and a blue whale, which weighs about 100 tons.

How did dinosaurs get such strange names?

The long, hard-to-pronounce names of dinosaurs all come from Latin words. Latin is the language that early scientists used to name living things. When modern scientists discover an animal or plant, they still give it a Latin name. That name is used by scientists all over the world, no matter what language they speak.

When dinosaurs were discovered, scientists gave them Latin names that described what each dinosaur was like. The words *tyrannosaurus rex* (ti-ran-uh-SORE-us recks) means king of the tyrant lizards. Nicknamed *T-rex*, this animal was a fierce, meat-eating dinosaur. The word *brontosaurus* (bron-tuh-SORE-us) means thundering big lizard. This dinosaur, a close relative of seismosaurus, was so big that the ground probably rumbled like thunder when it walked.

Which dinosaur had the smallest brain?

Stegosaurus (steg-uh-SORE-us) had a tiny brain—about the size of a walnut—even though the creature itself weighed nearly 30 tons!

Which dinosaur was the spikiest?

The spikiest of all the dinosaurs was kentrosaurus (ken-tro-SORE-us). This dinosaur had great big horns along its spine, from hips to tail.

Were there any flying dinosaurs?

No. There were no flying dinosaurs, but there were some flying reptiles called pterodactyls (ter-oh-DACK-tilz). None of these reptiles actually flapped their wings and flew like birds. Instead they all glided through the air, sailing along on the wind. Their wings were made of tough skin stretched between their long front legs and short back legs. One flying reptile had a wingspread of 27 feet!

PTERODACTYL

Which dinosaur had its own built-in fan?

Spinosaurus (spy-no-SORE-us) had a huge fan-shaped sail along its spine. Air flowing against the sail helped the animal keep cool.

What other reptiles lived in the days of the dinosaurs?

Quite a few water reptiles were around then. One of these was elasmosaurus (ee-laz-muh-SORE-us). It had a very long neck, and strong legs like flippers for swimming through the water.

Tylosaurus (tie-luh-SORE-us) was a sea reptile that looked something like a modern crocodile. It was a fierce animal with large jaws and very sharp teeth.

Archelon (AR-kuh-lon) was a giant water turtle. The biggest ones each weighed 6,000 pounds and were as long as a large car. Archelon looked very much like any turtle you might see today—except it was much bigger.

ELASMOSAURUS

TYLOSAURUS

ARCHELON

18

Although dinosaurs no longer roam the Earth, there are still lots of reptiles, large and small. Look around. You'll find reptiles in the zoo, or maybe even in your own backyard.

REPTILES AND SCALY THINGS

REPTILES

What kinds of reptiles are living today?

Today there are five kinds of reptiles. These are snakes, lizards, turtles, crocodiles and their relatives, and the tuatara (too-uh-TAH-ruh).

Why do reptiles stay underground in winter?

Because reptiles are cold-blooded animals, the temperature of their blood changes with the weather. When the air is warm, their blood is warm, too. When the weather gets cold, the temperature of their blood goes down. The reptiles can get too cold to stay alive. So, to keep from dying, they find a protected place to spend the cold days. They may stay in underground holes, in caves, or under rotting tree stumps. Even in these protected places, the reptiles are too cold to move. They lie still until the air warms up. Then they come outside again. Of course, when reptiles live in places that stay warm all year long, they never have to go underground—except to hide.

What is the tuatara?

The tuatara is a reptile left over from the days of the dinosaurs. All its closest relatives died a very long time ago, but the tuatara somehow survived in one part of the world—on islands near New Zealand.

The tuatara looks like an odd, big-headed lizard. It does everything slowly. It breathes only once an hour. Its eggs take more than a year to hatch, and a baby takes 20 years to grow up.

DON'T WORRY... NOTHING'S FOLLOWING US.

NATURAL HISTORY MUSEUM

REPTILE EXHIBIT

CROCODILES AND ALLIGATORS

Which is the biggest reptile living today?

The biggest reptile is the saltwater crocodile. This animal is usually about 14 feet long and weighs about 1,000 pounds. Some grow to 20 feet in length—the height of a two-story building!

What is the difference between an alligator and a crocodile?

The easiest way to tell the difference between an alligator and a crocodile is to look at their faces. The crocodile's face is long and pointy. The alligator has a shorter, wider face. When you see a crocodile bite down, its teeth interlock. When an alligator bites, its top teeth come down over its lower jaw.

CROCODILE

Do alligators and crocodiles eat people?

Yes, some of them do eat people. Almost any hungry crocodile or alligator may attack a person who comes close to it. But the African crocodile and the saltwater crocodile found in Southeast Asia and Australia are the most dangerous man-eaters. Hundreds of people are killed by these animals every year. American alligators and crocodiles usually leave people alone, though they have been known to attack people.

What does it mean when you say someone is shedding crocodile tears?

It means that the tears are not true, and the person doesn't feel sad. The saying probably comes from the fact that the shape of a crocodile's jaw makes it look as if it is smiling, even though it isn't. And if you can't trust a crocodile's smile, you also can't believe him if he cries.

21

 SNAKES

How long can a snake grow?

Some anacondas grow to be 25 feet long and 3 feet thick. That's about as long as seven bicycles lined up in a row!

Are snakes slimy?

Snakes are not at all slimy. In fact, their skins are quite dry, and they feel something like leather. People may think a snake is slimy when they see one sitting in the sun. When the sun shines on a snake, its skin looks shiny and almost wet.

Why do snakes stick out their tongues?

Snakes stick out their tongues in order to pick up smells and to feel things. Although many people think that a snake's tongue is a stinger, it is perfectly harmless.

WHEN YOU LIVE ON THE DESERT, YOU HAVE TO WATCH OUT FOR RATTLESNAKES...

A TWO-PRONGED STICK IS A GREAT DEFENSIVE WEAPON..

OF COURSE, YOU HAVE TO KNOW HOW TO USE IT...

Why do snakes shed their skins?

As a snake grows, its skin gets too small and tight for it, just as your shoes get too tight when your feet grow. So the snake grows a new skin and gets rid of—or sheds—the old one. The snake may do this three or four times a year.

How can a thin snake swallow a fat rat?

An amazing thing about snakes is that they swallow their meals whole. A snake's jawbones are attached very loosely so that its mouth can stretch very wide. The rest of its body can stretch, too, so a very big meal can fit inside. Large snakes can swallow whole rats and sometimes even whole pigs or whole goats! That's quite a meal.

Do snakes ever eat people?

None of the snakes that live in the United States are big enough to eat people. Most snakes eat only insects, mice, and other small animals. But there are two kinds of snakes that occasionally feast on a human being. Pythons (which can be found only in Asia and Africa) and anacondas (found only in South America) are the two man-eaters. These snakes are not poisonous. They kill their prey by wrapping themselves around it and squeezing it to death.

Are fangs like teeth?

Yes, fangs are hollow teeth with a tiny hole at the bottom. All snakes have teeth, but only poisonous snakes have fangs, too. When a fanged snake bites an animal, a poison called venom is forced through the fangs into the victim. A poisonous snake bites small animals in order to kill them for food. A snake bites people and other large animals only if it is scared and wants to protect itself.

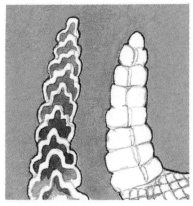

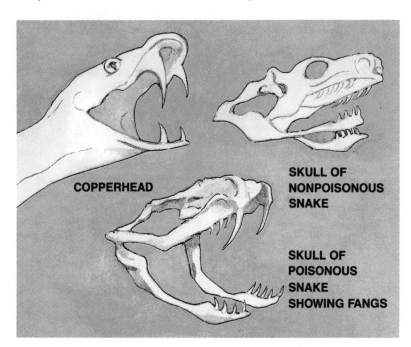

COPPERHEAD

SKULL OF NONPOISONOUS SNAKE

SKULL OF POISONOUS SNAKE SHOWING FANGS

How do rattlesnakes rattle?

At the end of a rattlesnake's tail are a few hard rings made of a material something like your fingernails. When the rattlesnake is excited, it usually shakes its tail. The hard rings hit against one another, making a rattling noise.

Are there poisonous snakes in the United States?

Yes, four kinds of poisonous snakes live in the United States. These are the rattlesnake, the copperhead, the water moccasin, and the coral snake. Of these four, the coral snake has the strongest venom. Fortunately, this snake is small and rarely bites anyone. The other three kinds of poisonous snakes have venom that would take a long time to kill a person. If a person gets bitten, he or she has enough time to go to a doctor and get an antivenom shot.

If you plan to be in an area where you might meet a dangerous snake, you can play it safe. People who hike and work in areas where there are poisonous snakes sometimes carry special medicine in a snakebite kit. You can, too.

24

Sonora Mountain king snakes look almost exactly like poisonous coral snakes, but they are harmless. Some people keep them as pets!

Can snakes really be charmed?

No. In India, men called snake charmers play music for cobra snakes, and the cobras seem to dance to it. But they are not really dancing. The snakes cannot even hear the music—they are completely deaf! The snakes can feel vibrations in the ground. A snake charmer taps his foot as he plays and sways in time to the music. A cobra feels the tapping, gets excited, and rears up, ready to strike him. When a cobra is ready to strike, it watches its victim carefully and follows the victim's movements. That's just what a cobra does with a snake charmer. The snake charmer is taking a big chance when he excites a cobra. Cobras have a deadly venom, but somehow snake charmers know how to keep an excited cobra from striking. Some snake charmers remove the cobra's fangs to be on the safe side.

HAWKSBILL
TURTLE

INDIAN STAR
TORTOISE

TURTLES

Is there any difference between a turtle and a tortoise?

Turtles live in the water, but some often come out on land. These are called terrapins. Other turtles—ones with flippers—spend most of their life swimming in the ocean. Tortoises (TORE-tus-uz) are large turtles that always live on land. However, we usually call both creatures turtles.

How long can a turtle live?

No one is sure how long turtles live, but some can probably live for a very long time—100 or maybe even 150 years.

How large can a turtle grow?

The largest turtle is the leatherback. It is a sea turtle that usually weighs between 600 and 800 pounds. The biggest one ever caught weighed nearly 2,000 pounds and was almost eight feet long.

Can a turtle crawl out of its shell?

No. The turtle's shell is attached to some of the turtle's bones.

The matamata turtle has wormy-looking bumps on its neck that fish try to eat. Instead, the matamata eats the fish!

Can you tell the age of a turtle by its shell?

By looking at its shell, you can tell the age of a young turtle, but not of an old turtle. The top of a turtle's shell is divided into sections. These are called shields. On each shield are little circles. In a young turtle, each circle stands for a year's growth. For example, a two-year-old turtle has two circles on each shield. After five or ten years, however, you can no longer find out the turtle's age by the circles. They have either become too crowded together or have begun to wear off.

LIZARDS

SALAMANDER

What is the difference between a lizard and a salamander?

Some lizards look very much like salamanders. However, the two animals are very different. Salamanders are amphibians. Most amphibians begin their life in water, breathing through gills like fish. Only after they have grown up are they able to live on land. Lizards, which are reptiles, are born with lungs. They always live on land.

Lizards have scales covering their bodies. Salamanders have smooth, moist skin without scales. Lizards love the sun, but salamanders do not. They stay away from it.

Can lizards grow new tails?

Some lizards can. The gecko, the glass snake, and the skink are three of the lizards that grow new tails. If an enemy catches one of them by the tail, the lizard can drop the tail and run away. Then the lizard grows a new tail. If only a piece of its tail is broken off, the lizard will sometimes grow back the missing piece and grow a whole new tail as well. So if you ever see a lizard with two tails, you'll know how it got them.

A gecko can clean its eyes with its tongue!

Are any lizards poisonous?

Only 2 out of about 3,000 known kinds of lizards are poisonous. One of these is the Mexican beaded lizard. The other is the Gila (HEE-luh) monster. The Gila monster lives in Mexico and in the southwestern United States. A bite from one of these two lizards can kill a person, but that rarely happens. The lizards don't usually put enough poison into people to kill them.

ARE YOU FOR REAL?

Do dragons really exist?

Dragons like the ones in storybooks do not exist. But there are huge reptiles like the creature Marcie is talking to called Komodo dragons. They live on Komodo Island and other islands in Indonesia. They are the largest lizards alive. These dragons can grow to be 10 feet long and weigh 300 pounds. They do not breathe fire, but they do like to eat. So watch out if you're ever near one!

Can lizards change their color?

Some lizards can. These include the anole, sometimes called the American chameleon (kuh-MEE-lee-un), and the true chameleons. They can turn different shades of brown and green. Their color depends on the amount of light hitting them, the temperature, and whether they are calm or scared.

A chameleon often turns the same color as its background to protect itself from enemies. A chameleon on a log, for example, may be brown.

A horned toad—a kind of lizard that lives in the desert—will squirt blood from its eyes when it's scared!

CHAMELEON

28

Have you ever wanted to soar through the air like a beautiful bird? It dips and circles and sails across the sky, but how does it do it? What's a bird's secret? Wings!

FEATHERED FRIENDS

ALL ABOUT BIRDS

What was the world's first bird?

The first bird was archaeopteryx (ar-ke-OP-ter-ix), which was about the size of a crow. It lived about 140 million years ago and was very much like a reptile. In fact, its ancestors *were* reptiles, and it is thought to be a bridge between reptiles and birds. Like a reptile, archaeopteryx had teeth and a long, bony tail, but archaeopteryx had feathers instead of scales. Also, the wings of the archaeopteryx were much like a modern bird's wings—with bones inside and feathers outside. But archaeopteryx couldn't fly very well. It couldn't flap its wings very hard. It probably used them more for gliding— sailing through the air.

How many different birds are there?

About 9,000 kinds of birds live on the Earth today. Birds can be found almost everywhere except the North and South Poles. The freezing temperatures in the Poles are too cold—even for penguins! There are more birds and different kinds of birds in Africa and South America than anywhere else.

How can you tell for sure which animals are birds and which aren't?

There's only one sure way to tell. See if it has feathers. If an animal has feathers, whether or not it can fly, it's a bird. Ostriches and penguins can't fly, but they are birds. If it hasn't got feathers, it's not a bird, even though it may fly—like bats or insects. All birds have two wings and two feet and no teeth. They have a hard mouth part called a bill or beak, which helps them catch and eat their food.

NOBODY HERE BUT US PENGUINS...

Why do birds have feathers?

Feathers help a bird keep warm. In cold weather, a bird fluffs up its feathers and traps a layer of warm air under them. The fluffed feathers act like a blanket by holding in body heat. In warmer weather a bird squeezes its feathers against its body to let body heat escape.

Feathers also help a bird fly. In flight, a bird uses its outer wing feathers to move forward in the air. Wing feathers and tail feathers are both used for balancing, steering, and braking.

Do all birds eat worms?

No. Different kinds of birds eat different kinds of food. Usually birds have favorite foods, but will eat some other things, too. Many birds like worms and insects best. Birds that live near water often eat fish or shellfish. Owls, hawks, and eagles eat fish and meat—mice, rabbits, smaller birds, snakes, and other animals. Many small birds, such as sparrows, live on seeds. Some birds eat mostly fruit and berries. Hummingbirds like to drink the sweet liquid called nectar that is found in flowers.

Why do woodpeckers peck at trees?

Woodpeckers peck at trees to get food. They eat insects that live in the trees, just under the bark. Most woodpeckers also peck out nesting holes in trees.

WHO?

Does an ostrich really stick its head in the sand to hide from an enemy?

No, an ostrich isn't that stupid. What this tall bird does is fall down flat when it sees danger in the distance. An enemy may not spot the ostrich in this position, or it may think the ostrich is just a bush. As soon as danger comes near, however, the ostrich will take off and run. Although an ostrich cannot fly, it can run as fast as 40 miles an hour.

Are owls really wise?

Owls are no wiser than many other birds. In fact, some birds are smarter. But owls have large, staring eyes, which make them look as if they are thinking very hard. That's probably why people started calling them wise.

Nests and Eggs

How do birds learn to make nests?

Birds don't learn to build nests. Nest building is an instinct. Each kind of bird is born knowing how to build its own kind of nest. Many birds make a cup-shaped nest out of twigs and grass. Cardinals and thrushes make this kind of nest. Some swallows make their nests in a hole in a tree or rock. They line the bottom of the hole with grass, feathers, fur, and moss. Certain weaverbirds make complicated "apartment-house" nests out of stems. This system of nests may be ten feet high and hold a hundred or more birds.

Do all bird eggs look like chicken eggs?

Most eggs are shaped the same as chicken eggs, but they have different sizes and colors. Large birds lay large eggs, and small birds lay small eggs. The colors of eggs vary from one kind of bird to another. The eggs often blend in with the colors around the nest so an enemy can't spot them easily. Eggs may be light blue, brown, white, gray, or green. A few are red or pinkish orange. Some eggs are spotted or speckled.

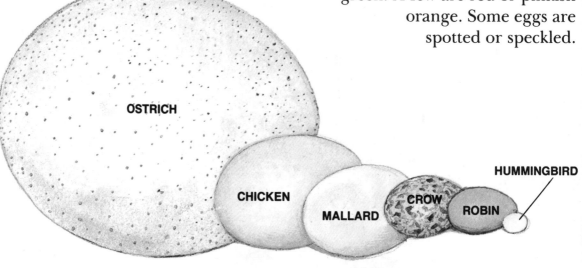

OSTRICH
CHICKEN
MALLARD
CROW
ROBIN
HUMMINGBIRD

Which bird lays the smallest egg?

A hummingbird—which is the smallest bird—lays the smallest egg. Its egg is only about half an inch long.

Which bird lays the biggest egg

The ostrich—which is the biggest bird—lays the biggest egg. This egg can be as long as 8 inches and can weigh up to 4 pounds.

If a 250-pound animal sat down on an ostrich egg, the egg would not break! This is because the egg has a special oval shape that makes it hard to break.

Why do birds sit on their eggs?

Birds sit on their eggs to keep them warm. When an egg is kept warm, the baby bird inside can grow and then hatch, or come out of the shell.

BIRDS IN FLIGHT

Why can birds fly?

A bird's body is specially built for flying. It is very light. There are pockets of air in it, and most of the bones are hollow. So a bird doesn't have to lift much weight into the air. A bird has very strong muscles for flapping its wings, and the wings have just the right shape for flying. The inner part of a bird's wing is like the wing of an airplane. It lifts the bird up in the air. The outer part of the wing acts like a propeller. Its long feathers pull on the air and move the bird forward. The design of airplane wings was copied from birds' wings.

Some birds will fly upside down to attract a mate!

I THINK WOODSTOCK IS IN LOVE AGAIN !!

Are there any birds that can't fly?

The ostrich, the cassowary (KASS-uh-wer-ee), the rhea (REE-uh), the emu (EE-myu), and the kiwi (KEE-wee) are all nonfliers. They have wings, but their flying muscles are not strong enough to be useful. But they are very fast runners. Penguins also can't fly. They have wings like flippers, which they use to swim and dive powerfully. Chickens cannot fly very well, but they can flutter around a bit.

How can a hummingbird stand still in the air?

A hummingbird can stay in one spot in the air, or "hover," because it can beat its wings very fast—from 55 to 90 times in one second! Its wings move so fast that they look like a blur. A hummingbird hovers in front of flowers when it drinks nectar.

Hummingbirds can fly backwards!

Every year Arctic terns fly 11,000 miles south to Antarctica and 11,000 miles back home again. That's 22,000 miles each year!

Some birds live far out over the ocean and almost never land on the ground!

Where do birds go in winter?

Before winter comes, many birds that live in the north fly south, where the weather is warmer. In the spring, they fly north again. We say that those birds "migrate." No one is sure why birds began migrating, but the need for food was probably the main reason. In cold places there are few insects, flowers, fruits, and seeds around for birds to eat. Ponds and streams are frozen over, so fishing birds cannot get food, either. In warm places, food of all kinds is available.

TO THE SLOPES

BIRD SONGS

Why do birds sing?

Bird songs are not just pretty music. Birds usually sing to tell other birds of their kind to keep away from their nesting area. Often birds sing to attract a mate. Sometimes they seem to sing just for the fun of it.

Do all birds sing?

No. Female birds rarely sing, and only about half the males have songs. But nearly all birds give calls. Calls are short, simple sounds. The *whoo-whoo* of an owl is a call. So is the *cluck-cluck* of a hen.

Calls are often used to express alarm and warn other birds of danger. Birds "talk" to their babies with calls. Baby birds use calls to say they are hungry.

PROTECTING BIRDS

How do birds protect themselves?

Birds protect themselves by always listening and watching for danger. At the smallest sign of it, they will fly away. Birds that cannot fly are often able to swim fast, or run quickly and kick, too. Some birds—such as owls—make themselves look dangerous by fluffing out their feathers. Other birds will hiss at enemies and scare them away.

Another important protection for many birds is their color. Their feathers often have colors that match the things around their nest. Some birds, such as the ptarmigan (TAR-muh-gun), change colors with the seasons.

Why have some birds become extinct?

Some kinds of birds have become extinct because people have killed all of them. The dodo, the passenger pigeon, the great auk, and the Carolina parakeet are some of the birds that have become extinct. Hunters have killed birds for their colored feathers, their oil, or their meat. Today some farmers kill larger birds that sometimes eat small farm animals.

People also kill birds without meaning to. When people cut down forests and fill in swamps to build houses and factories, they destroy the homes and the food of birds. If the birds have nowhere else to go and nothing to eat, they die out.

Pollution may soon cause some birds to become extinct. Birds that eat fish from polluted water get poison in their bodies. Then they can't lay healthy eggs. New birds aren't born.

36

If you could take a peek into the past, you'd see more than just dinosaurs. Other creatures roamed the Earth millions of years ago. They were the world's first mammals.

INCREDIBLE CREATURES FROM LONG AGO

WHAT IS A MAMMAL?

What is a mammal?

A mammal is an animal that drinks milk from its mother's body when it is a baby. No other animals do this. Most baby mammals grow inside their mother's belly before they are born. Most other animals grow inside eggs that their mother lays.

All mammals are warm-blooded. This means that their body temperature always stays about the same. And they are the only animals that have hair or fur. (Some insects are fuzzy, but they don't have real hair.) Most mammals have four legs, or two arms and two legs.

Dogs are mammals. So are cats, giraffes, bats, cows, horses, rats, monkeys, and dolphins. You are a mammal, too.

THE FIRST MAMMALS ON EARTH

When did the first mammals appear?

The first mammals appeared about 180 million years ago. They probably looked like shrews or rats, having long, pointed snouts and long tails. There were few kinds of mammals on Earth at first, but there were many dinosaurs. As these huge reptiles began to die out about 65 million years ago, many new kinds of mammals appeared on Earth. In a way, these creatures were early versions of dogs, cats, elephants, and horses.

EOHIPPUS

What was the earliest horse?

The ancestor of the horse—the eohippus (ee-o-HIP-us)—was about the size of a small dog. Instead of hoofs, it had three toes on each hind foot and four toes on each front foot. Over millions of years, the horse grew to the size it is now.

Did dogs and cats live on Earth long?

About 25 million years ago, the first doglike and catlike animals appeared. Some of the cats developed into large, fierce animals. One was the saber-toothed tiger. It was about the size of a modern tiger, but two of its front teeth were very long—about eight inches!—and very sharp. Even the largest animals were probably scared of it.

What was a woolly rhino?

One of the earliest mammals was a rhinoceros. It started out small, but as millions of years passed, it became larger. Huge groups of these rhinos moved north to cold lands and grew thick coats of hair. These rhinos were called "woolly" rhinos.

There were also woolly mammoths. They appeared about two million years ago and became extinct only about 10,000 years ago. Mammoths were related to elephants. They were very large and had long, thick hair. Scientists know exactly how they looked, because whole mammoths have been found frozen in ice.

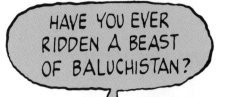

HAVE YOU EVER RIDDEN A BEAST OF BALUCHISTAN?

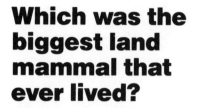

Which was the biggest land mammal that ever lived?

The beast of Baluchistan (buh-loo-chih-STAN). This huge animal looked something like an overgrown rhinoceros. It died out about 20 million years ago. The animal could grow as large as 37 feet long and 25 feet tall. It weighed as much as 22 tons. One of its legs alone was much larger than a grown man!

COLLECTING MAMMAL FACTS

How do we know about early mammals?

We know about them because people have found stone fossils of their bones and teeth in the earth. People have also found real bones and teeth in large pits of tar in La Brea, California. About one million years ago, thousands of animals sank into these tar pits and died. The tar hardened and kept their bones almost perfectly. The bones were very easy to dig out and to study. Saber-toothed tigers, mammoths, vultures, snakes, and camels were some of the animals found in the La Brea tar pits.

Many mammals have also been found frozen in the ice in the far north. Just the way a freezer keeps food from spoiling, the frozen ice kept whole animals from rotting away for hundreds of thousands of years. Many woolly mammoths and woolly rhinos have been found in ice.

A record of animals that lived about 40,000 years ago was left by early people. They painted pictures of animals on cave walls.

CHAPTER 5

Mammals live in almost every part of the Earth—from the coldest to the hottest, the driest to the wettest, on land, in the air, and underwater. There are millions of mammals everywhere—and they do some amazing things!

MEET SOME MAMMALS FROM A TO Z

FOLLOW THE ALPHABET TO SOME OF YOUR FAVORITE MAMMALS

What mammal can live in the coldest climate of all?

The **arctic fox** is comfortable at temperatures as low as 45 degrees below zero. This small white fox seems to be better equipped than even polar bears to manage well in sub-freezing weather.

Are bats really blind?

No. **Bats** can see. In fact, some see very well. However, bats come out mostly at night and many of them have a hard time seeing in the dark. These bats use their ears to help them get around. The bats make little clicking sounds. They can tell by the echo how near or far away an object is. Bats have wings that they can flap, so they are the only mammals that can fly.

How do beavers build dams?

Beavers have four very sharp front teeth. With these teeth, they cut down trees, then cut the trees into pieces. The cut logs and branches are used to make their dams.

A family of beavers usually works together to build a dam. They make a base of logs across a narrow part of a stream. They weigh it down with rocks and branches, then fill the holes with mud. A finished dam is about three or four feet high. It makes a perfect home for beavers, because the deep water around the dam keeps enemies away.

Most bats sleep hanging upside down!

I HATE PLAYING "BAT"!

One group of beavers built a dam more than 2,000 feet long. That's longer than the Brooklyn Bridge in New York City!

Do bulls really attack when they see red?

No, they don't. Bull-fighters always wave a red cape in front of a bull, but the color red is not what makes the bull charge. In fact, the bull is color-blind. He cannot see red or any other color. But the bull sees the movement of the cape and gets excited.

Why do camels have humps?

Camels live in the desert. They sometimes have to go for a long time without any food. That's when their humps become useful. The humps are made of fat. The camel can get its energy from this fat if it has no food. When the camel has not eaten for a few days, its humps get smaller. They get big again after the camel has filled itself up with food.

Why do a cat's eyes shine at night?

A cat's eyes shine because they reflect light. Even in the darkest night, there is usually some stray light from a streetlamp or the headlights of a car. A cat's eyes reflect this light because they have a special coating on them. The coating helps the cat see in the dark, and also makes the cat's eyes shine.

House cats are not the only cats with eyes that reflect light. Jaguars, lions, tigers, leopards, and all other cats have eyes that shine at night.

What is the world's fastest mammal?

The fastest mammal is a wildcat called the cheetah. It can run at more than 60 miles an hour, and sometimes as fast as 70 miles an hour. But the cheetah can keep up this speed for only a short distance. Then it slows down.

Cougar, puma, panther, painter, mountain lion, catamount, American lion, and Indian devil are all names for the same kind of wildcat!

CHEETAH

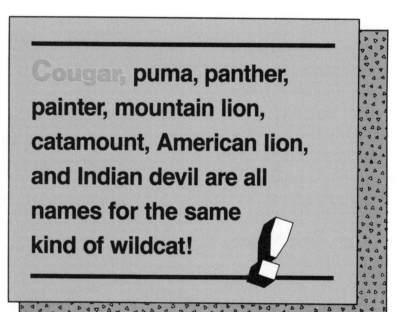

Which mammal is most like humans?

Chimpanzees are built a lot like us. They often walk on two feet the way we do, and they have no tail. However, chimps have longer arms, shorter legs, and a more hairy body than we do. The chimpanzee is probably the smartest animal next to man. Some chimpanzees have learned to say and understand a few English words. Others have learned to use the sign language of the deaf. By using sign language, chimpanzees have been taught to answer questions that scientists ask them, solve problems, and even express their feelings.

Chimps also have their own language. They make at least 20 different sounds "talking" to one another.

Why does a cow keep chewing when it isn't eating?

A **cow** has a special stomach with four parts. When it eats some grass, it chews just enough to make it wet. Then the grass goes into the first part of the stomach, where it becomes softer. From there it goes into the second part, where it is made into little balls called "cuds." Later, while the cow is resting, it brings up each cud one at a time and chews it well. When the cow swallows it, the food goes into the third part of the cow's stomach. There the water is squeezed out of it. Finally the food goes to the fourth part of the cow's stomach and is broken down into very tiny pieces. Then the cow's body can take what it needs from the food to live and grow.

Earth's first space traveler was a dog!

Panel 1: HOW ABOUT GOING FOR A NICE WALK?

Panel 2: IT'LL SHOW EVERYONE WHAT GOOD FRIENDS WE ARE...

Panel 3: AS WE WALK DOWN THE STREET, PEOPLE WILL SAY, "LOOK, THERE GOES A BOY AND HIS DOG!"

Panel 4: I'M GLAD HE WARNED ME!

Why do dogs pant?

Dogs pant to cool off when they are feeling hot. People cool off by sweating, but dogs don't sweat very much. Instead, they breathe hard, with their tongues hanging out. This brings air into their bodies. The air cools their insides.

Why does a dog wag its tail?

Tail-wagging is one of the ways that a **dog** "talks." You know that a dog is feeling happy when it wags its tail at you. Dogs also use tail wags to give special messages to other dogs. One kind of wag means, "Hello. Glad to see you." Another means, "I'm the boss around here." A third means, "Okay, you're the boss."

How does an elephant use its trunk?

An **elephant** uses a trunk as a nose, hand, and arm. The elephant uses its trunk to smell, to feel along the ground, and to pick up objects. At the tip of its trunk it has either one or two "fingers," which can pick up something as small as a peanut. With its whole trunk, it can lift something as large as a tree!

An elephant also uses its trunk to show affection. A mother pets her baby with her trunk. Both males and females pet each other with their trunks during mating season.

An elephant can also suck up water with its trunk. It drinks by spraying the water into its mouth. Sometimes it sprays water all over its back. This shower keeps the elephant cool and clean.

47

What is the tallest mammal?

With its long neck and long legs, the giraffe is the tallest animal in the world. Its head may be 19 feet above the ground. The giraffe's height helps it in two ways. First, the giraffe can easily see a great distance over the flat open land where it lives. If a hungry lion is anywhere near, the giraffe will spot it soon enough to run away. Second, the giraffe can eat the leaves high up on trees. Other animals cannot reach these leaves, so the giraffe doesn't have to worry about missing out on a good meal!

Can groundhogs really predict weather?

No, they can't. Groundhogs, also known as woodchucks, hibernate all winter in a hole in the ground. The story goes that on February 2—Groundhog Day—the groundhog comes up out of its hole. If the day is cloudy and the groundhog can't see its shadow, the cold days of winter are over. If the groundhog sees its shadow, the animal returns to its hole. Then we are supposed to have six more weeks of cold weather.

The story is fun, but there is no truth to it. Groundhogs stay in their holes until the weather warms up enough for them to come out. This may happen much later than February 2, or even earlier. Once outside, groundhogs don't look for shadows. They just go about their business—which is *not* predicting the weather!

Why does a kangaroo have a pouch?

A female **kangaroo** has a pouch so that her baby will have a place to live. When a kangaroo is born, it is only about an inch long—skinny, hairless, and very helpless. It is not ready to live in the outside world. So it crawls across its mother's body and into her pouch. There it can keep warm and safe and drink its mother's milk.

The baby kangaroo stays completely inside its mother's pouch for about six months. Then it begins to stick its head out to eat leaves from low branches. When the baby kangaroo is about eight months old, it jumps out of its mother's pouch for good. Although the young kangaroo is big enough to walk around, its mother still watches it. She pulls it back into the pouch when danger is near.

If you annoy a **llama**, it will spit in your face!

A BABY EAGLE IS CALLED AN EAGLET

A KANGAROO IS A JOEY.. A CODFISH IS A CODLING...

WHAT DO THEY CALL A BABY BROTHER?

PATHETIC!

© 1987 United Feature Syndicate, Inc.

2-26

Is a pony a baby horse?

No, a baby horse is called a foal. A **pony** is a kind of horse that just happens to be small. When fully grown, it is between 32 and 58 inches tall. It weighs less than 800 pounds. That doesn't seem very small until you compare a pony to other horses. A large workhorse can weigh more than 2,000 pounds!

Can porcupines shoot their quills?

No, but their quills are sometimes found stuck in other animals. That's probably how the "shooting" story got started. Actually, **porcupine** quills come off the porcupine very easily. Its tail is particularly full of loose quills. When another animal attacks, the porcupine swings its tail at the enemy. Quills are driven deep into the enemy's flesh. The enemy runs off in pain. Animals that attack porcupines learn their lesson very quickly and don't bother porcupines ever again.

A possum uses its tail to hang from a tree.

What does "playing possum" mean?

The expression "playing possum" comes from a habit of an animal called the **possum**, or opossum. It falls over limp, as if it were dead, whenever danger is near. This act protects the possum. Most meat-eating animals like to kill their own meals. They are not interested in an animal that lies still and already seems to be dead.

People used to think that the possum purposely played a trick on its enemies by pretending to be dead. But now we know that the possum passes out when danger is near. It is not playing at all.

What is the smallest mammal?

The smallest mammal is the **pygmy** (PIG-mee) **shrew**, a small, mouselike creature, which when full grown weighs about half an ounce. These little animals are big eaters, though. A shrew can eat up to three times its body weight every day.

When the spotted skunk gets ready to spray, it stands on its front legs with its back ones in the air!

Why do skunks give off a bad smell?

Skunks give off a bad smell to protect themselves from enemies. When a skunk is angry or frightened, it shoots an oily spray into the air. This bad-smelling spray comes from two openings near the skunk's tail. If the spray hits the face of an animal, it burns and stings. It also tastes terrible.

NEVER GET ON THE WRONG SIDE OF A SKUNK!

What is the largest mammal?

The blue **whale** is the largest mammal that has ever lived. It can reach more than 100 feet in length (the height of a 10-story building) and weighs almost 150 tons. That's more than 300,000 pounds. What does this giant whale eat? Small shrimplike creatures called krill.

Why is a whale called a mammal?

A **whale** lives in water and has a fishlike shape and no legs. But a whale is not a fish. It is a mammal, and it acts like one. A whale—like other mammals—grows inside its mother, is born alive, drinks milk from its mother's body, breathes air through lungs, and is warm-blooded. Like all other mammals, the whale has some hair and no scales. A fish, on the other hand, usually hatches from an egg, does not drink milk, breathes underwater through gills, is cold-blooded, and usually has scales.

Why does a zebra have stripes?

A **zebra's** stripes help it hide from enemies. When you see a zebra in the zoo, its stripes make it stand out clearly. But normally the zebra lives in places where there is very tall grass. The zebra's stripes blend in when it stands in the shadows of the blades of grass. The perfect hiding place!

CHAPTER 6

There's nobody else exactly like you. But you do have one thing in common with every person in the world. You're a member of the human race—a marvelous mammal.

WHERE DO YOU FIT IN?

THE FIRST PEOPLE ON EARTH

When did the first people appear on Earth?

What do scientists call us? Human beings like us are called *Homo sapiens*. Our nearest relatives are believed to have existed between 30,000 and 70,000 years ago. They were named Cro-Magnon people.

Scientists say Cro-Magnon people looked very much like us. Some were over six feet tall and had unusually large brains. Many bones and partial skeletons of Cro-Magnon people have been found in caves such as the Lascaux cave in France. The caves also contain tools, sculpture, and paintings that give us an idea of the skills and artistic abilities of Cro-Magnon people. The nearest relatives of Cro-Magnon people are believed to have been Neanderthal people, who originated about 150,000 years ago. Neanderthal people were short, powerfully built, without chins. Still, in spite of their apelike appearance, scientists think Neanderthal people were intelligent.

THE FIRST PEOPLE IN AMERICA

When did people first come to America?

Scientists think that the very first men and women came to this part of the world between 7,000 and 12,000 years ago. They probably started their journey in northern Asia. After crossing a narrow passage in the sea called the Bering Strait, they probably entered the part of North America that is now Alaska.

ARCTIC OCEAN

BERING STRAIT

BERING SEA

ALASKA (USA)

N
NW · NE
W · E
SW · SE
S

People have been on Earth about 30,000 to 70,000 years. Compare this to cats, who have been here for about 8,000,000 years!

RHINOCEROS

There are more than 1,000,000 species (kinds) of animals. Insects account for 800,000 species. All the rest of the animals make up the remaining 200,000 species.

Animals in Danger

Some animals have disappeared from the Earth. They are extinct. Many others also are now in danger of dying out.

No California condors exist free in the world. They are all in zoos. The giant panda and the mountain gorilla are in danger of dying out. And because of game hunters, African elephants and black rhinoceroses are almost extinct.

With the help of zoos and international wildlife groups, many people are working hard to protect endangered animals. They would like to keep these creatures alive, healthy, and free.

Be a Mammal Detective

If you study tracks in the ground or snow in your neighborhood, you might be able to find out what animals live there. It will take a little practice, but soon you'll be able to learn the differences among the tracks of a bird,

SNOOPY

YOU'VE BEEN A DOG ALL YOUR LIFE, HAVEN'T YOU?

© 1989 United Feature Syndicate, Inc.

I'VE OFTEN WONDERED WHAT MADE YOU DECIDE TO BECOME A DOG..

8-16

I WAS FOOLED BY THE JOB DESCRIPTION

squirrel, dog, cat, mouse, and rabbit. Skilled trackers can even tell the difference between the tracks of a black bear and those of a grizzly bear.

Happy Birthday, One and All!

Different animals are likely to live different amounts of time. This list shows that some have surprisingly long and short life spans.

SPECIES	LIFE SPAN
• mayfly	a few hours
• rat or mouse	2 to 3 years
• garter snake	5 to 6 years
• rattlesnake	14 to 18 years
• dog and cat	12 to 15 years
• parrot, swan, and goose	50 years
• alligator	50 years
• elephant	60 to 70 years
• human beings	70 to 85 years
• tortoise	100 to 150 years

People used to live about 70 years. Today, thanks to good diet and health care, the average life span has increased. Some people live through their 80s—and some even get to blow out 100 candles on their birthday cake!

PELICAN

GOOSE

EAGLE

WOODPECKER

WOODSTOCK

Does It Fit the Bill?

You can tell what kind of food a bird eats by looking at its bill. Seed-eating birds usually have short, stubby beaks—just right for cracking open seeds. The woodpecker's larger bill makes it easy to bore into trees and dig out insects. The eagle is a meat-eater. Its hooked beak helps it tear its food into bite-sized pieces. And the pelican uses the large pouch under its beak like a fishing net for scooping up fish.

Name That Scientist

People who study animals are called zoologists (zoe-AHL-uh-jists). Scientists who study certain types of animals have special names. Here are a few:

SCIENTIST	SUBJECT
entomologist (en-tuh-MAHL-uh-jist)	insects
herpetologist (her-pih-TAHL-uh-jist)	reptiles
ichthyologist (ik -thee-AHL-uh-jist)	fish
ornithologist (or-nih-THAHL-uh-jist)	birds

Talking Animals?

Most animals express themselves, but not with words the way people do. They use movements, smells, and sounds. A kitten meows to its mother to let her know that it's hungry. A bird chatters or sings to warn other birds to keep away from its nest. Some scientists think that dolphins may be able to actually talk to one another!

The Nose Knows

Some mother animals find their babies by their smell. When a baby is born, its mother sniffs it and re-members the scent. From then on, when-ever the mother wants to find her baby, she will sniff at all the babies until she finds the right one.

Sleepy Time

Many animals sleep all winter. Animals like ground squirrels, woodchucks, and jumping mice can't find food when the weather gets cold. So they eat a lot and grow very fat before winter comes. Then they sleep—or hibernate (HIGH-ber-nate)—in-side a deep hole. They can live all winter on fat stored up in their bodies. When spring comes, warm weather and hunger wake up the sleepers. It's time to stretch and find a tasty meal!

Z

◆ I N T H E ◆

NEXT VOLUME

Have you ever wondered how it feels to blast off in a spacecraft, or who was the first space traveler, or why your weight drops to zero in outer space? You can find these answers and lots more in volume 3, *Blast Off to Space—Astronauts, Rockets, and Moon Walks.*